P9-BIK-110

Kings Lived in Castles

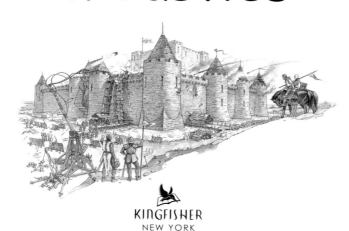

KINGFISHER
NEW YORK

Copyright © Kingfisher 2012
Published in the United States by Kingfisher,
175 Fifth Ave., New York, NY 10010
Kingfisher is an imprint of Macmillan Children's Books, London.
All rights reserved.

Written and designed by Dynamo Ltd.

Distributed in the U.S. and Canada by Macmillan,
175 Fifth Ave., New York, NY 10010

Library of Congress Cataloging-in-Publication data has been applied for.

ISBN 978-0-7534-7010-7

Kingfisher books are available for special promotions and premiums. For details contact:
Special Markets Department, Macmillan, 175 Fifth Ave., New York, NY 10010.

For more information, please visit www.kingfisherbooks.com

Printed in China
9 8 7 6 5 4 3 2 1
1TR/0612/HH/-/140MA

Contents

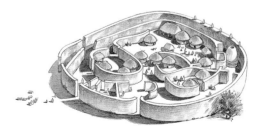

When were castles built?

Most castles were built between roughly 1,000 and 500 years ago, in a time called the Middle Ages.

They were built around Europe and the Middle East as strongholds for kings and nobles.

All about castles

- It took up to 20 years to finish a castle.
- More than 2,000 people might have been needed to build a castle.
- They worked on wooden platforms high above the ground.

Castles were built
out of stone

The stone
carvers were
called masons

Why did kings live in castles?

Kings ruled in the Middle Ages. They controlled their kingdoms from their castles.

Castles were safe places to stay. They were very hard for an enemy to attack.

Kings in the Middle Ages

- Kings usually had more than one castle.
- They traveled between their castles with their soldiers and servants.
- Kings made all of the laws in the Middle Ages. Anyone who disobeyed his or her king could be killed.

Kings were safe
inside their castles

The king's
servants all
lived there, too

7

What was it like to eat at a castle feast?

The main room in a castle was called the great hall. Big feasts were held there on special occasions.

Servants brought in many different kinds of food, while musicians played for the guests.

At the feast

- Diners drank wine or beer because water was dirty and full of germs in the Middle Ages.
- The castle owner and his family would sit at a special table, higher than everyone else.
- Leftover bones were thrown on the floor for the castle dogs.

Many different courses
were served at feasts

There were no
forks—only
spoons and knives

People ate
with their
fingers

9

What was thrown out castle windows?

In the Middle Ages, people threw their dirty water and garbage out the window.

In a castle, the garbage went into the moat or a hole called a cesspit. In a town, people threw garbage onto the street.

Medieval toilets

- There were no flushing toilets at this time.
- Castle toilets were just holes in the wall leading down to the moat.
- In ordinary houses people used a pot for a toilet and threw the slops out.

People outside
had to watch out!

11

What did people wear in castles?

Rich people had their clothes made for them. Poor people made their own clothing.

Wealthy people wore the most expensive clothes and jewelry. They followed the latest fashions.

Castle clothes

- Kings and queens wore the finest clothes of all.
- Royal clothing might have had jewels and pearls sewn onto it.
- Poor people wore plain, simple clothes.

Ladies wore
long dresses

Men wore
robes or tunics

13

What was the best way to capture a castle?

To capture a castle, the enemy had to find a way in. They might try battering a hole in the wall, or climbing up the side.

They used battering rams and giant catapults to try to damage the castle walls.

Attacking a castle

- The people inside a castle fired arrows at the enemy.
- They sometimes poured boiling oil down onto the attackers below.
- They pulled up the drawbridge to stop anyone from getting across the moat.

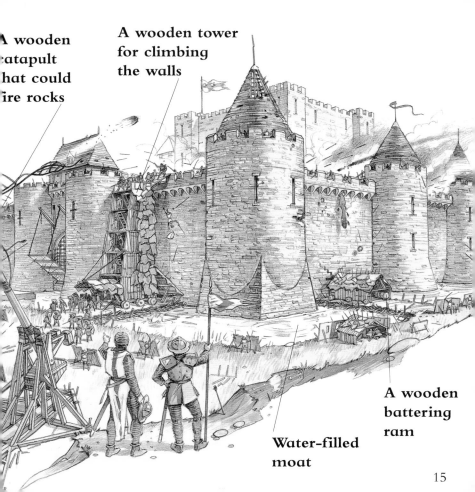

A wooden catapult that could fire rocks

A wooden tower for climbing the walls

A wooden battering ram

Water-filled moat

15

Why did knights try to knock each other over?

Competitions called jousts were sometimes held near castles. The castle knights competed for a prize.

They galloped toward each other and tried to knock each other off using long wooden poles called lances.

All about knights

- Knights served under kings or important nobles.
- They fought battles wearing metal armor.
- Their horses were big and strong, like modern draft horses.

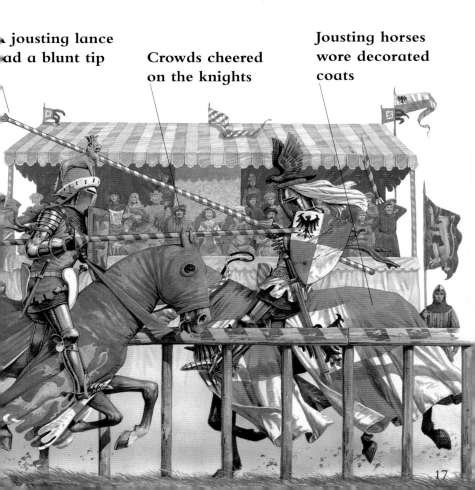

A jousting lance
had a blunt tip

Crowds cheered
on the knights

Jousting horses
wore decorated
coats

17

Who lived outside a castle?

Towns sometimes grew up around castles. In the town there were houses, workshops, and food markets.

Some towns had their own walls and gateways to keep enemies out.

A castle town

- Farmers brought their food to sell in towns.
- They traveled by horse and cart.
- They sold the food in the town market.

A town gate

A farmer's
cart

A soldier
guarding
the gate

What happened to castles?

At the end of the Middle Ages, people started using big guns called cannon. They fired cannonballs that could blow up castle walls.

People started to fight wars differently, so castles were no longer important.

The end of castles

- A castle was a cold and uncomfortable home.
- Kings went to live in more comfortable palaces.
- Battles were fought between big armies on battlefields, not around castles.

Many castles were left empty, and they fell down

Castle remains can still be seen in Europe

21

What do you know about castles?

You can find all of the answers to these questions in this book.

Did castles have flushing toilets like we have today?

What jobs do you think servants did in castles?

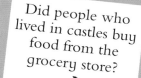

Did people who lived in castles buy food from the grocery store?

How would you try to batter down a castle wall in a battle?

Would you like to live in a castle?

When knights jousted, what did they do?

Some castle words

Catapult A machine that can throw something hard. Giant catapults were used to throw rocks at castles.

Cesspit A smelly hole in the ground where garbage was dumped.

Great hall The biggest room in a castle, where feasts were eaten.

Joust A competition between knights, who tried to knock each other off their horses.

Lance A long pole used as a weapon.

Mason Someone who carved stone.

Moat A deep, water-filled trench dug around a castle.